TWO WOMEN, THREE FLAMINGOES AND A POOCH

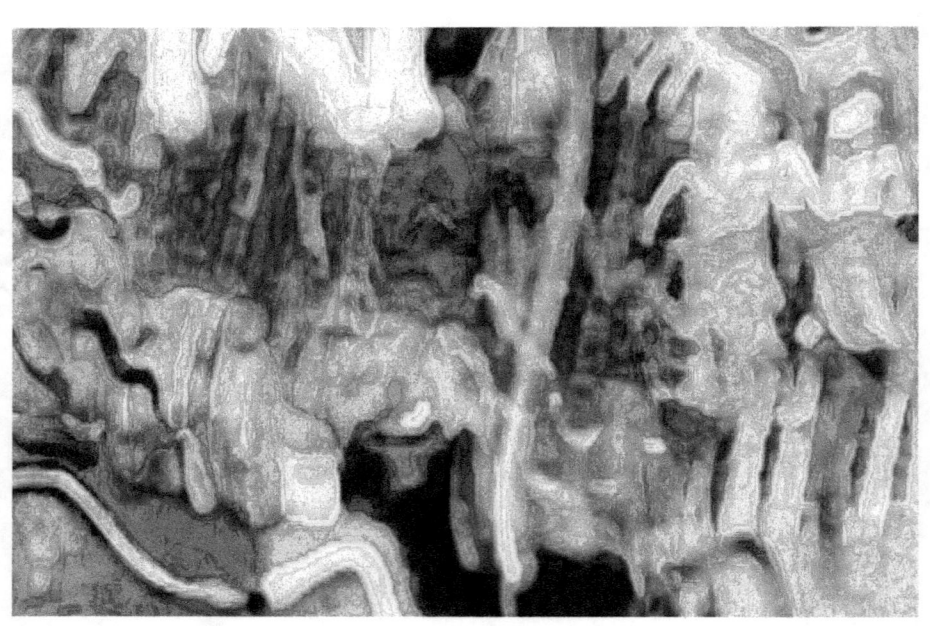

TWO WOMEN, THREE FLAMINGOES AND A POOCH

PRINT OPERAS BW

BY

MISHA HA BAKA

TWO WOMEN, THREE FLAMINGOES AND A POOCH
Print Operas BW

ISBN-13: 978-0-9987941-4-3
ISBN-10: 0-9987941-4-7

Published by Ha Baka Book

Although every precaution has been taken to verify the accuracy of the information contained herein, the author and publisher assume no responsibility for any errors or omissions. No liability is assumed for damages that may result from the use of information contained within.

First edition paperback 2017

DEDICATION

For Mothers,

Their Sons

And

Their Daughters.

Print Operas BW

Operas of the Soul

As a child, I picked up some pastels and began sketching flowers. As a teenager, I turned to the camera and started doing photography. I picked up a guitar or synthesizer and started to compose, or picked up some brushes and started to paint. Over the years this creativity has manifested itself as photography, music, painting, writing, healing and as of late cooking and baking.

Simultaneous to a driving fascination with ancient philosophies was an attraction to state-of-the-art technologies. I strove to experiment with the innovative technological advances as they came forward. With painting, the medium used always communicated its *intelligence* to me by instructing me how to use it to express both it and myself. Oils taught me fluidity, color, brilliance, and longevity; gauche and watercolors taught me patience and precision; Sumi-e taught me speed and tonality; pastels taught me transitional gentleness, and ink drawings taught me exactitude and delineation. However, it wasn't until I was able to waltz with the digital camera that I experienced freedom.

The camera was the brush, and light was the medium. This light danced across my electronic canvas as I played my inspirational compositions. Then I was faced with the creative choice: How can I take a fluid dancing moment and translate that to a stationary print? After much experimentation, these digital paintings were created. My intent was to produce a print, which stretched the gamut of color intensity and captured the luminosity, brilliance, and multi-dimensionality of the original digital art. To this end, I juxtaposed graduated, delineated, linearity against the vibrating, intense, blended color fields to create what I call *Print Operas*.

We art what we are. When I look at the Print Opera series, I can see the technology, the healing energetics, the music, the dance, the luminosity of gems, and the brilliance of metals. All of these echo elements of my experience. It was also much to my surprise when I began to see other things in them too. The seemingly random moments in time and space when synthesized together appeared to whisper and hint at archetypal shapes, dimensional forms and even some stories unfolded. At first, I thought I was creatively fantasizing, but when others, without prompt saw such too, I knew this was not a subjective experience.

Receptive viewers were entranced by the art experience, as they were absorbed into the Print

Opera sequence. They found the experience to be an opportunity of heightened visual excitement coupled with being momentarily transported to a space outside their own. Subsequent viewings were opportunities for the discovery of previously unseen new aspects. For me stationary, visual art is a mini-vacation. Like watching a film, you leave your present circumstances and travel elsewhere, even if only for a few moments. The more successful the work, the longer you can stay in it and revisit it over and over again. After having created these works, it was much to my surprise and pleasure to see that so many of the diverse influencing aspects of my life could come together in the way that they did.

I look at these works as synchronistic coincidences, which happen to synergistically integrate to produce archetypal inferences. I see them as being simple, complex, bold, dynamic, and deep. I used whatever state of the art computer, video, and photographic technology available to me to create an encapsulated amalgamation of a dance of light.

These artworks are signed and meticulously self-published on fine art paper using gicleé with inks rated high for permanency and are faithfully reproduced in this book. They are also for sale as unsigned reproductions on canvas, on board or paper.

The creative process was not only a joy to participate in, but it also visually confirmed there was design inherent in randomness. Perhaps it was the principles of tossing coins to randomly obtain a hexagram in the I Ching, the Chinese Book of Changes that first inspired me to randomly select images to create the Print Operas. Perhaps it was the mathematical binary exactitude, the basis of computers also inherent within the very same book that gave me the original concept of melding technology with art. In 1982 I was inspired to produce computer-generated color art using only a black ink dot matrix printer, a computer, and specially self-designed media. Years of working with more traditional mediums and media gave me the foundation to break free of using exacting equipment in an exact manner.

A dream which began in the '70s, that of creating art with music, lead me down my path to have a motion/rhythm palette to choose from. I trusted the creative process to allow my art to be a true expression of the diverse influencing aspects of my life. Print Operas BW resonate and vibrate. They dance and take flight like music. They soar using the highest and lowest ranges of tones and shades and they delve and dive deeply into the collective consciousness bringing forth energetic statements of ancient themes with futuristic echoes. They are *Operas of the Soul*. This volume is the black and white version of this book.

Two Women, Three Flamingoes and a Pooch Print Operas BW

The first two volumes of the Print Opera series of digital paintings were *Two Women Contemplating the Nature of the Universe: Print Operas BW (black and white) Volume 1* and *Print Operas (Color) Volume 2*. This is Volume 4 and is titled, *Two Women, Three Flamingoes and a Pooch: Print Operas* BW. It is the black and white version of the book. Volume 3 is the color version of the book and is titled, *Two Women, Three Flamingoes and a Pooch: Print Operas*.

Abstract art is just that – abstract. However, it is *fun* to see the *stract* in the "ab-stract." While I was creating the series, my two women made an encore performance in a new painting. When I looked at the original painting of *Two Women Contemplating the Nature of the Universe*, I was surprised to see what appeared to be two figures in the lower left-hand corner looking up at the rest of the painting. They looked female. This time they reappeared in the lower right-hand corner of the painting and brought along three flamingoes and their pooch. It looks like they enjoy walking around. Perhaps it is a multi-colored cocker spaniel? In the previous volumes these *two women,* (I will let your imagination run wild as to their identity.) shared their unbridled opinions on the paintings in a humorous manner. For this volume, they respectfully requested to assume a serious demeanor. After all, they did not want you the reader to walk away thinking that everything is a joke. So herein they convey their sincere and serious thoughts and feelings about this new series of Print

Operas. But then again, what is serious to some may be quite humorous to another…

Thank you for visiting my literary art gallery yet again. For the first time visitor, you are invited to visit Volumes 1 and 2 of *Two Women Contemplating the Nature of the Universe*. And most importantly *seriously* – speaking. Enjoy.

Misha Ha Baka 2017

TWO WOMEN,
THREE FLAMINGOES
AND A
POOCH

Two Women, Three Flamingoes and a Pooch

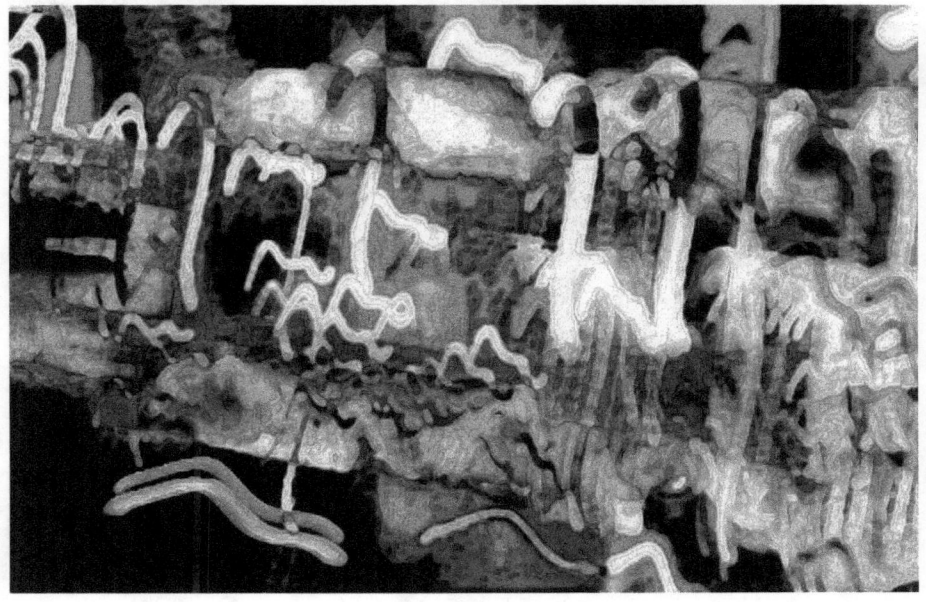

"I am delighted that we finally made it to the right side of things."
"You are most probably right, but what do we do with what is left?"

CHINOISE

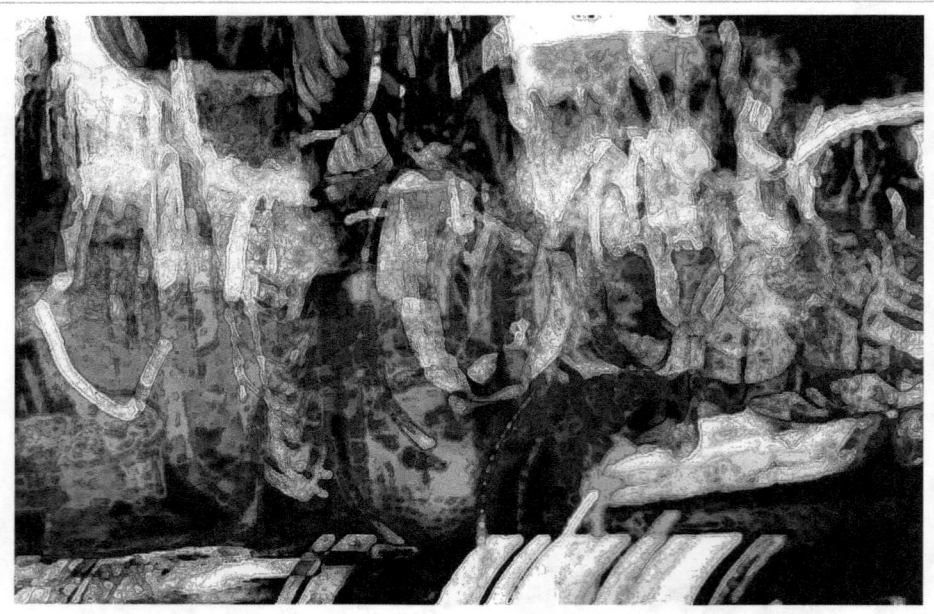

"I have no idea what that *Chinoise* means, do you?"
"Of course, *Chinoise* is French for your double chin."

HERD

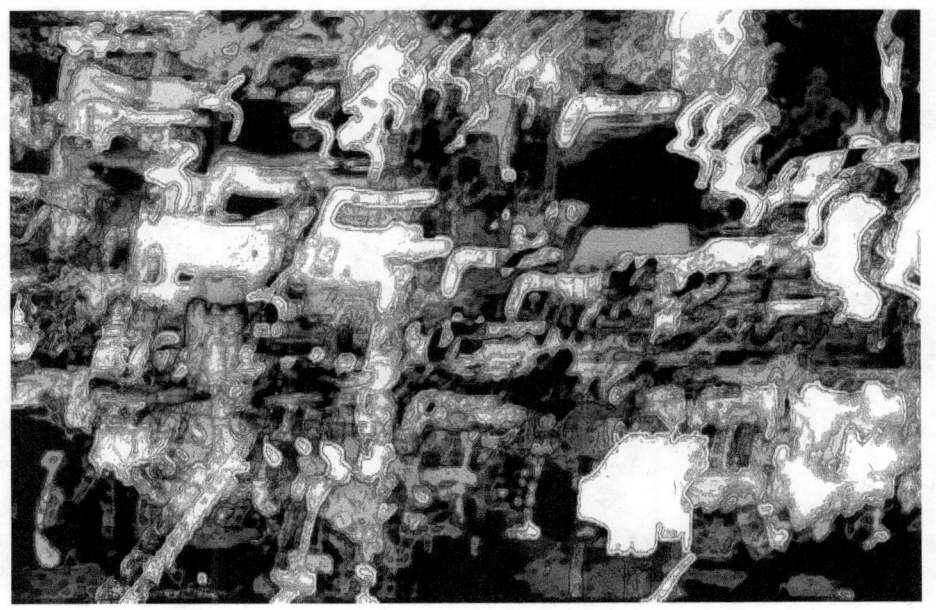

"I am an independent thinker and neva' follow the *herd*."
"Me too! I don't believe everything I heard also."

JUNGLE SUNRISE

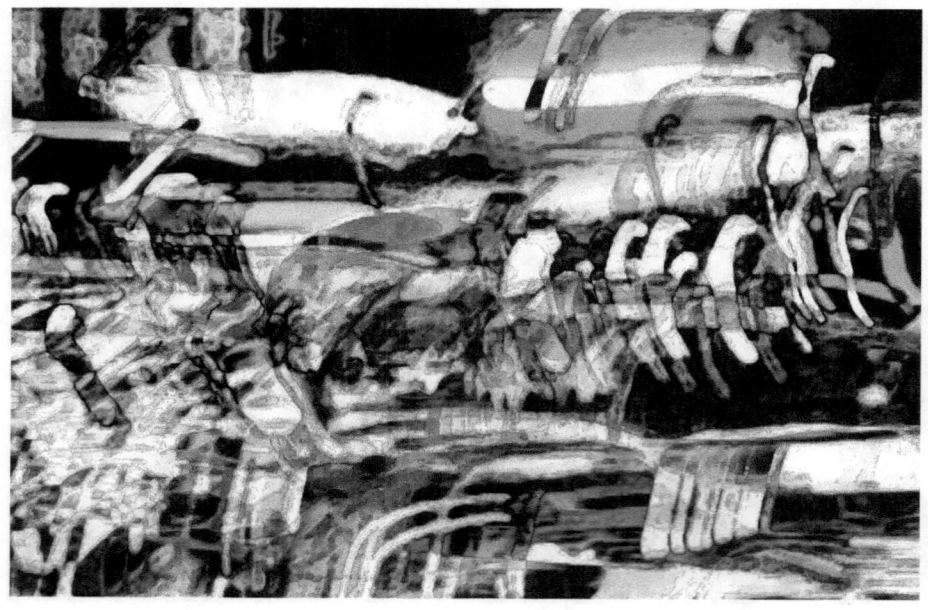

"Do you ever see a jungle sun?"
"Yesterday the sun shined into my closet, and it was a jungle in there!"

TREE OF LIFE

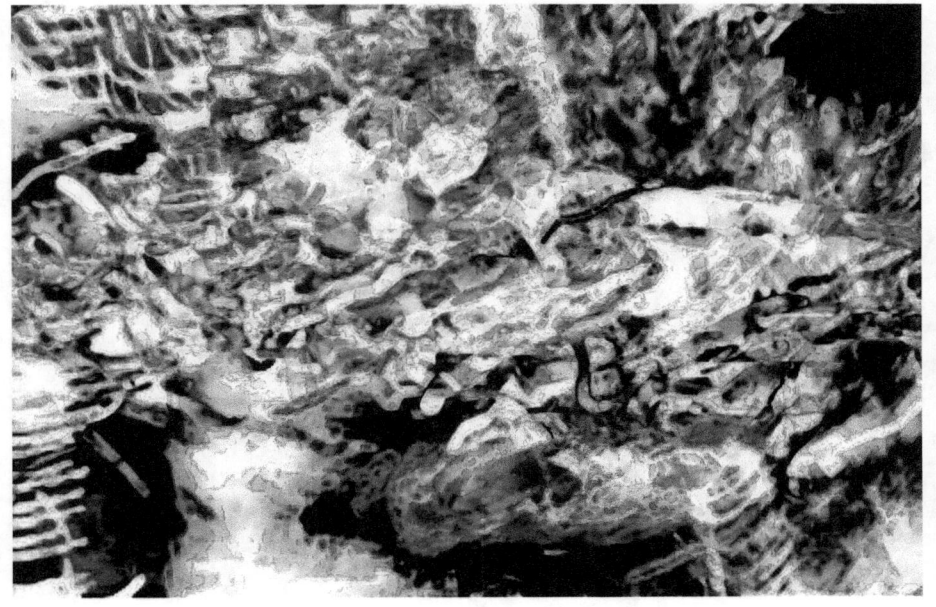

"You know that we got a bad *rap* over this!"
"Organic apples are supposed to be good for you, 'No?' "

METROPOLIS

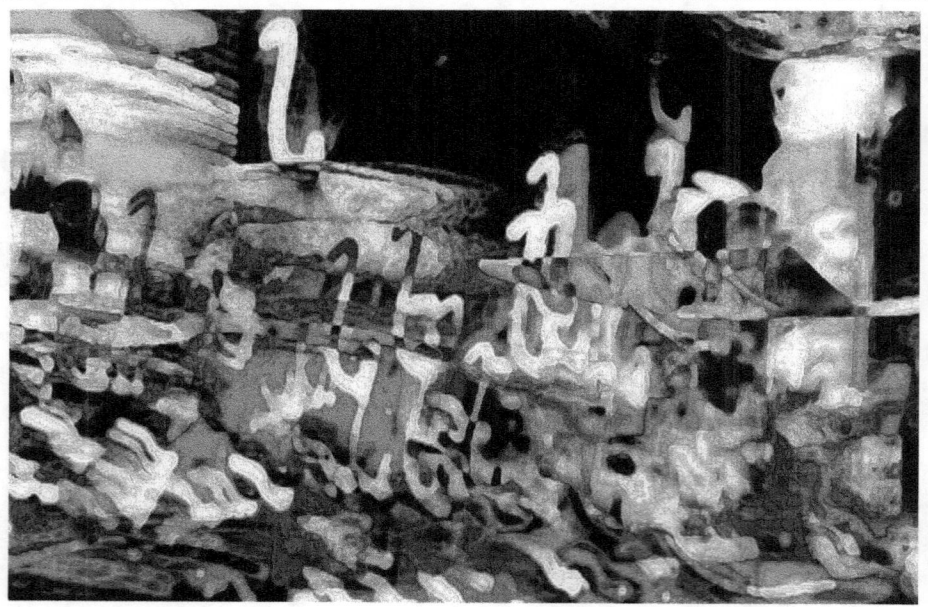

"I am happy that they finally built some cities."
"Yes, I was tired of shopping for clay potties."

Extravagance

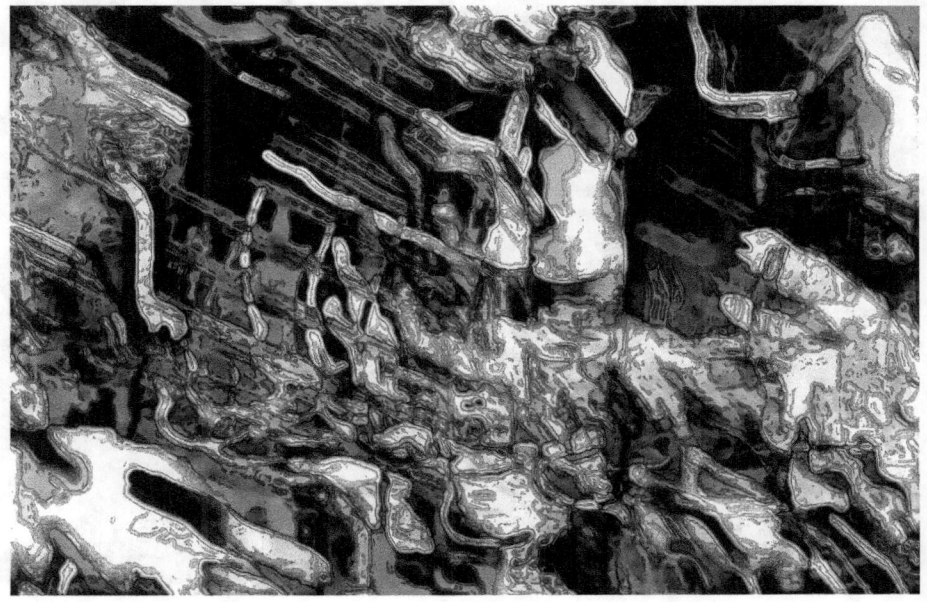

"I'm happy to be able to buy whatever I need even before I need it."
"True, your shoe closet gives new definition to the word *endless*."

EXERCISE

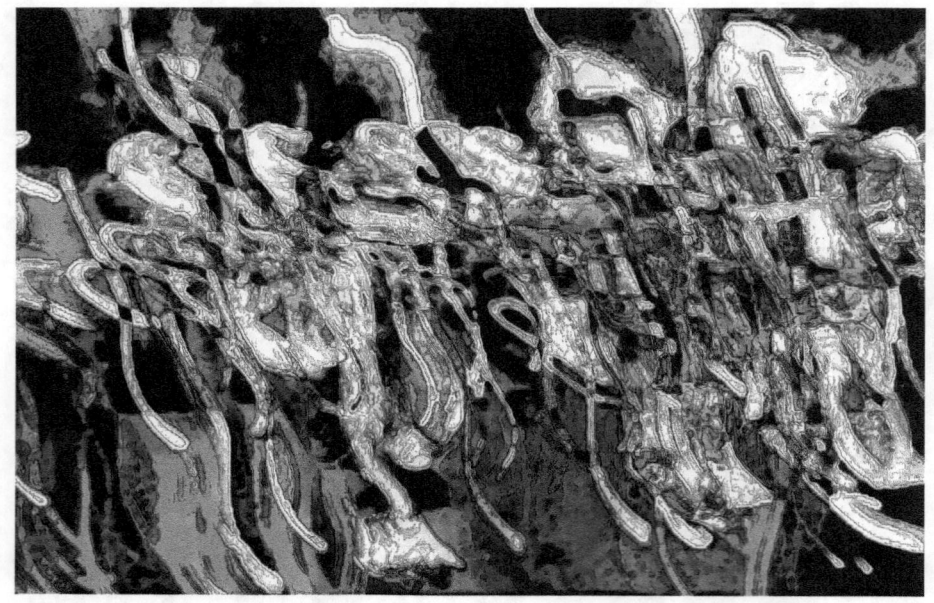

"Why do they give it a man's name?"
"Honey, it's called a *Gym*, not *Jim*."

COMMERCE

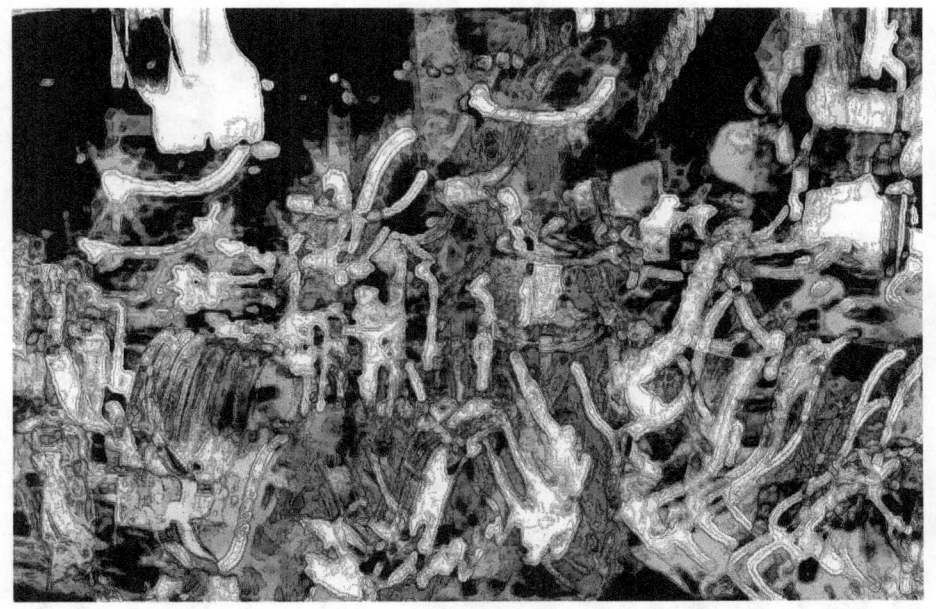

"Whoever invented money was a genius."
"Spending money you don't have on credit is the true genius."

CITYSCAPE

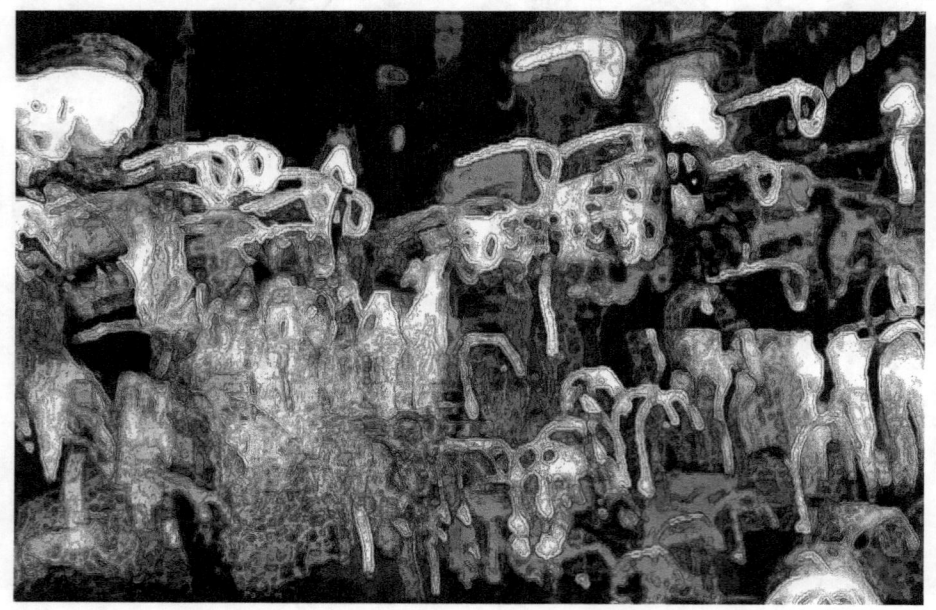

"I love going for a stroll in the city."
"Raising your hand for a taxi and getting in is *not* a leisurely stroll."

ABUNDANCE

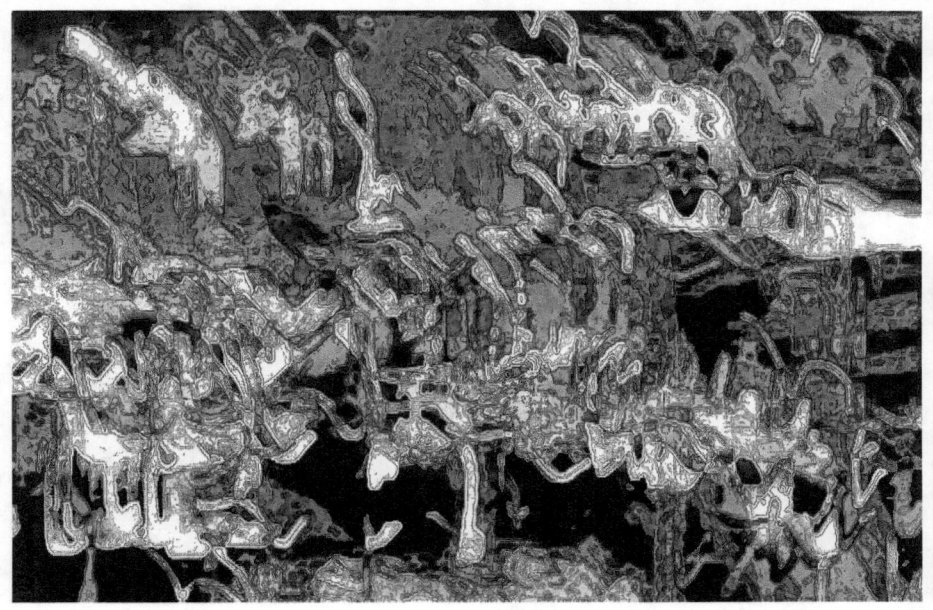

"If I already have everything I need, why do I want even more?"
"Because you also *needed* to want more?"

RUSH HOUR

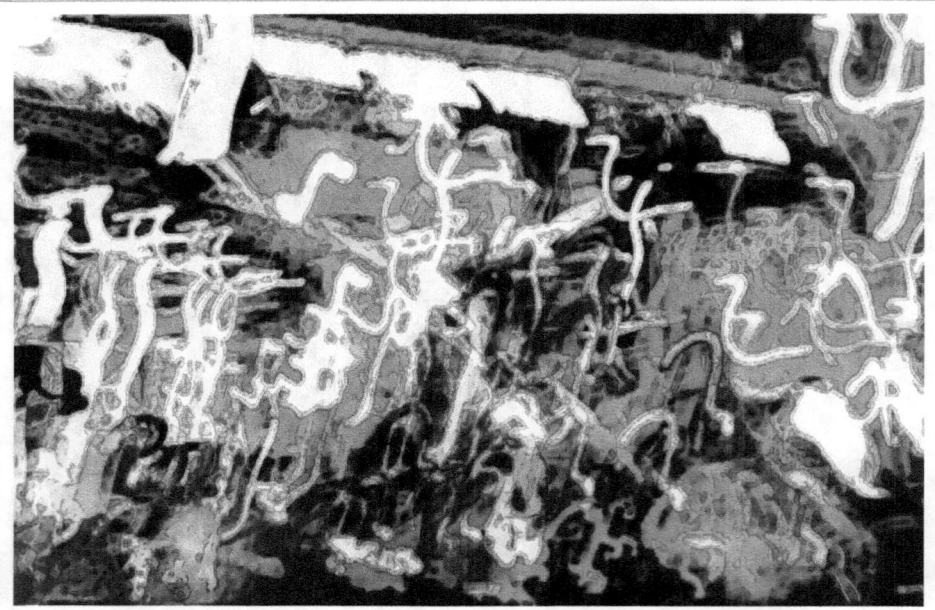

"Do people who live more than an hour away still rush to work?"
"No, they have more than an hour to get there."

TRAPEZE

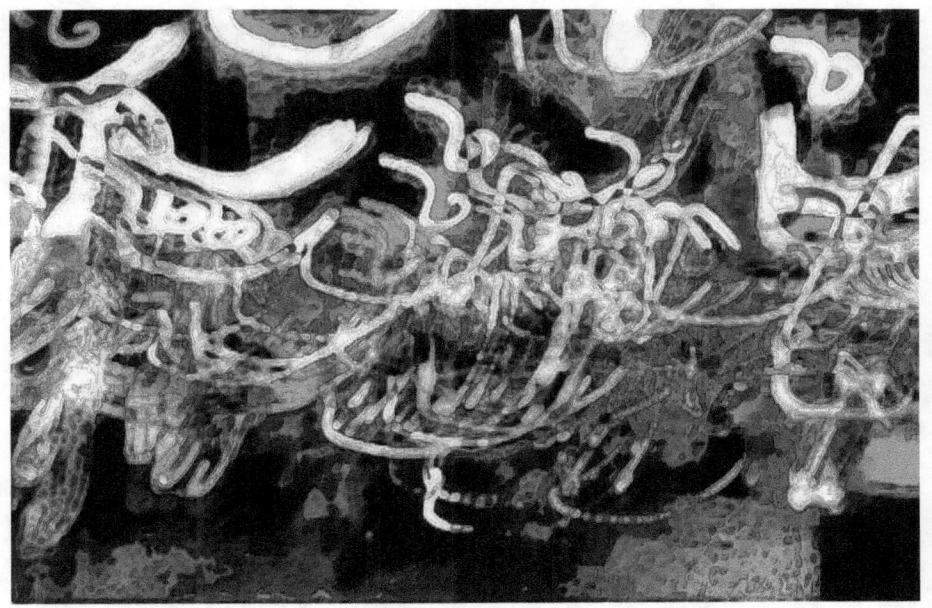

"Do you ever feel like you are being swept away by life?"
"Yes, when I'm in the hammock and the wind blows too strong."

ELYXR

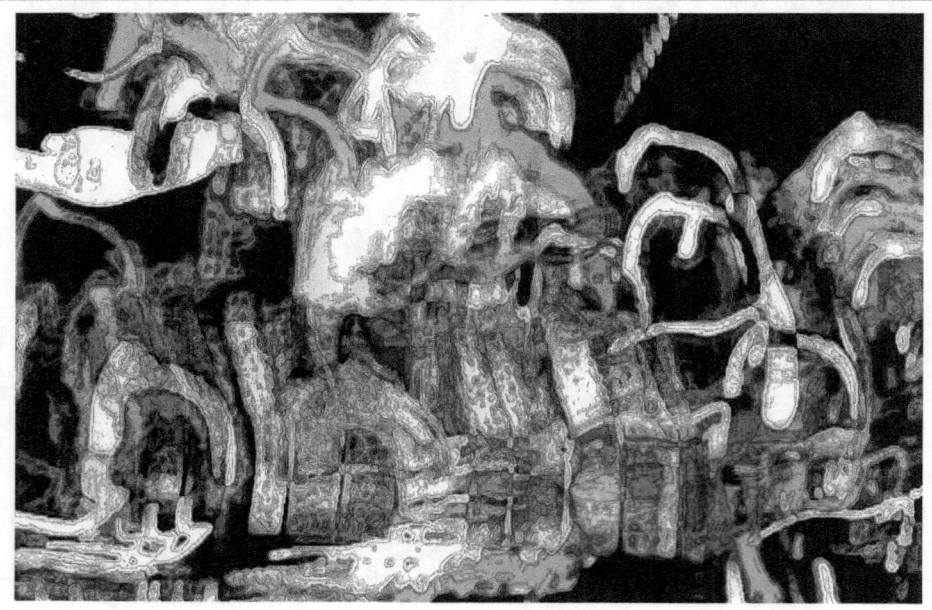

"I think I can live a thousand years on thick shakes."
"Putting fiber in some water will send you to the potty, not Nirvana."

DRAGON

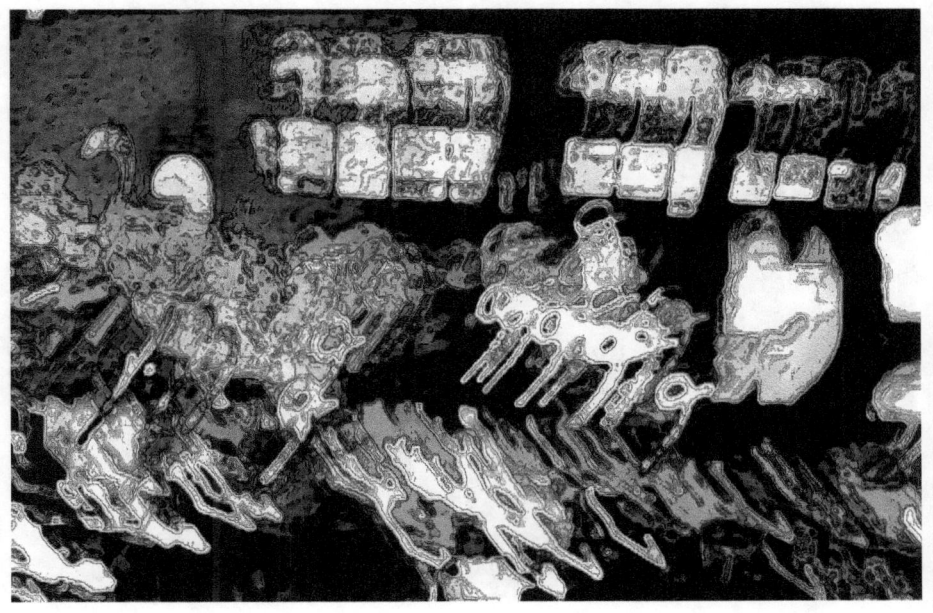

"I may have some hidden dragons in my closet."
"Forget about ever finding them, your closet is way too full."

DIMENSION

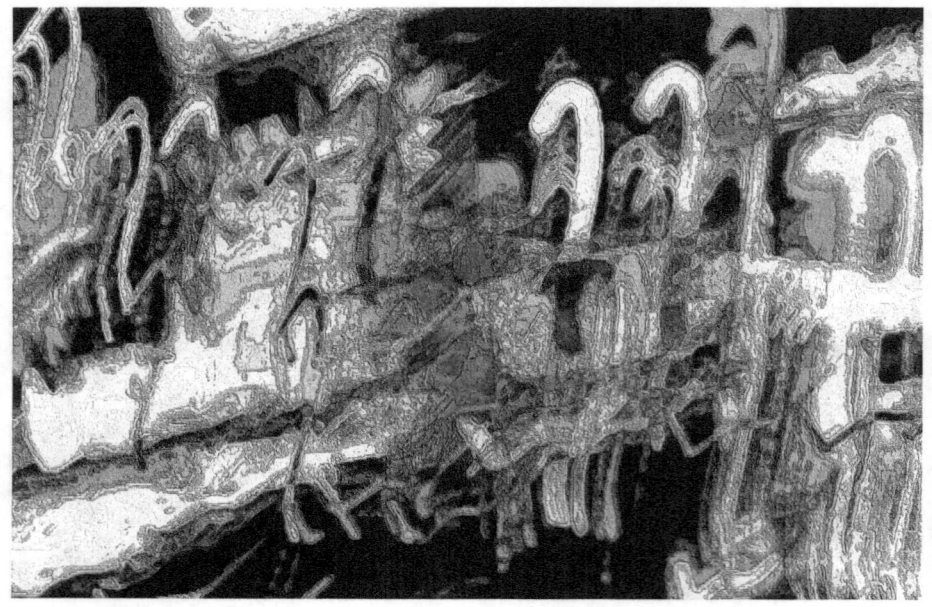

"Do you think that there are other *me's* in parallel dimensions?"
"One *you* is too much to handle, more *yous* would be incomprehensible."

Thrust

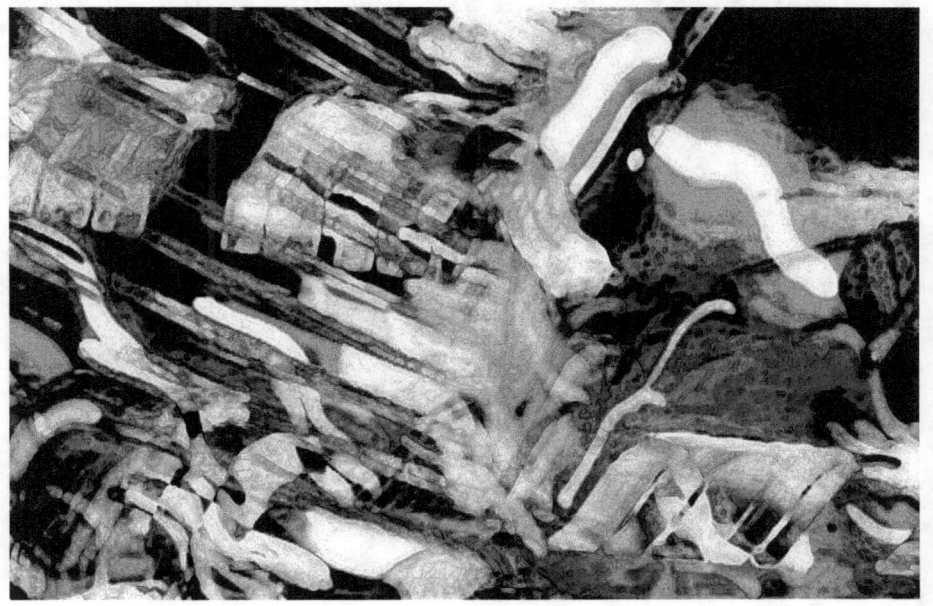

"Do you think I think about men too much?"
"No, if you can't be with one then thinking is the next best thing."

PEGASUS

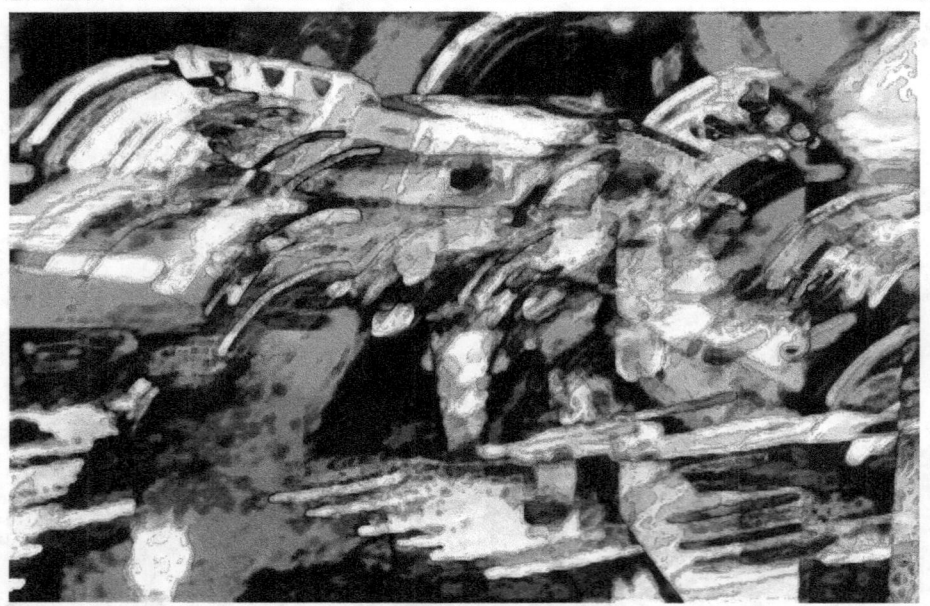

"Do you believe in mythical creatures?"
"There are no such things as *mythical* creatures; they really exist."

ANGELS

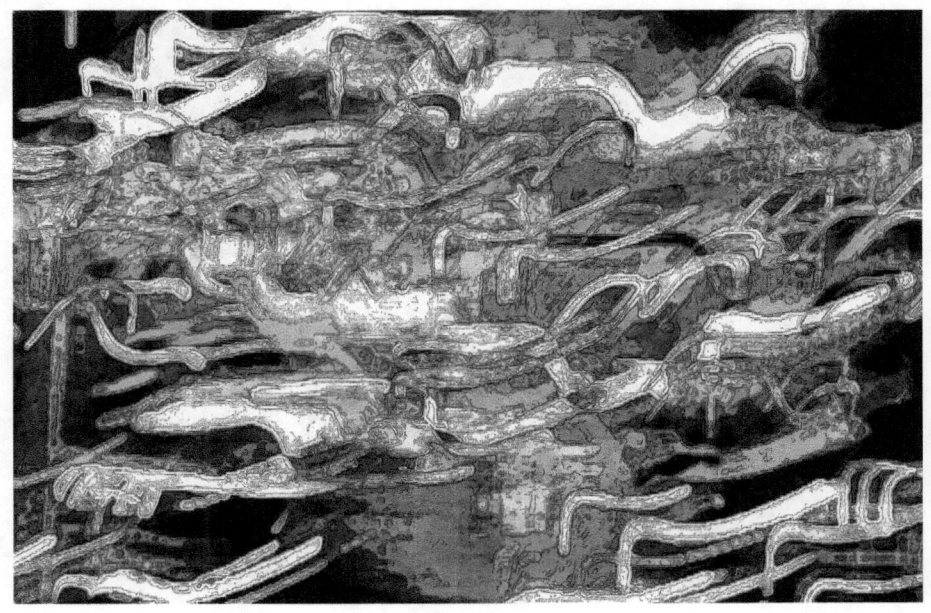

"I have a guardian angel."
"Your *Sugar Daddy* doesn't count as being a *real* angel."

ALCHEMY

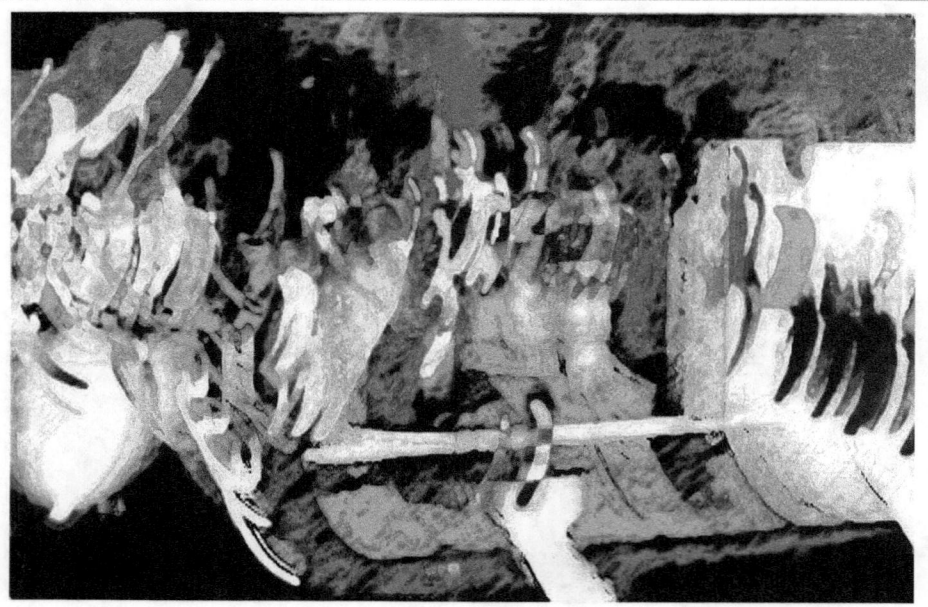

"My money seems to disappear before I even spend it?"
"You are a modern-day alchemist who can turn gold into nothing."

CELEBRATION

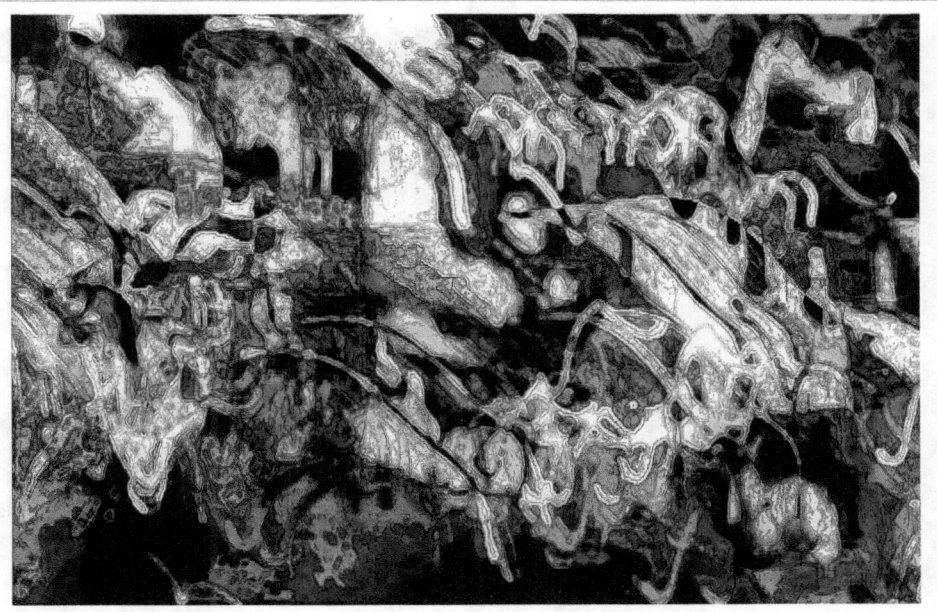

"I feel holy personages deserve our reverence and respect."
"For once we agree. Amen."

CURRENT

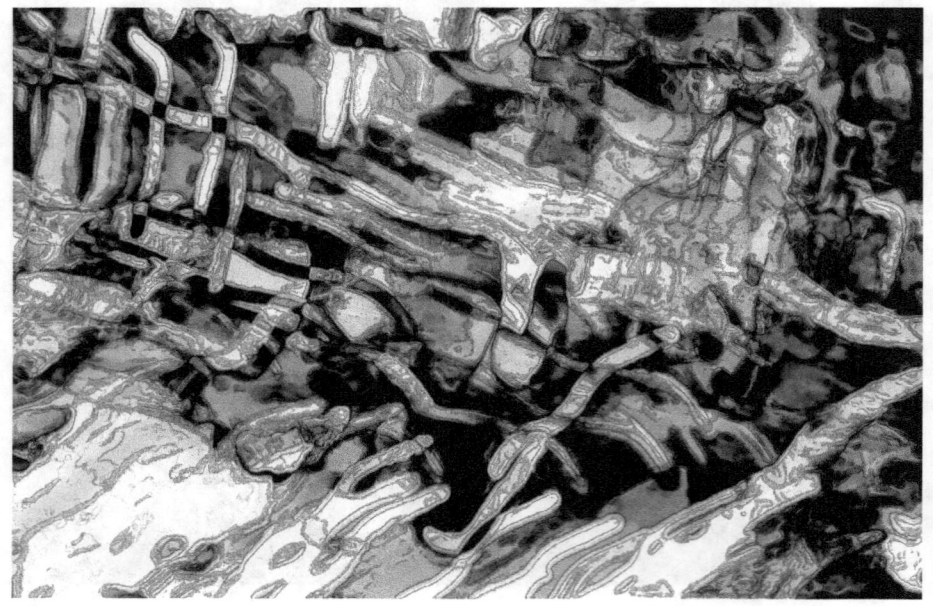

"I went with the *flow* once."
"A ferry around Manhattan is not considered as going with the *flow*."

SYNCHRONICITY

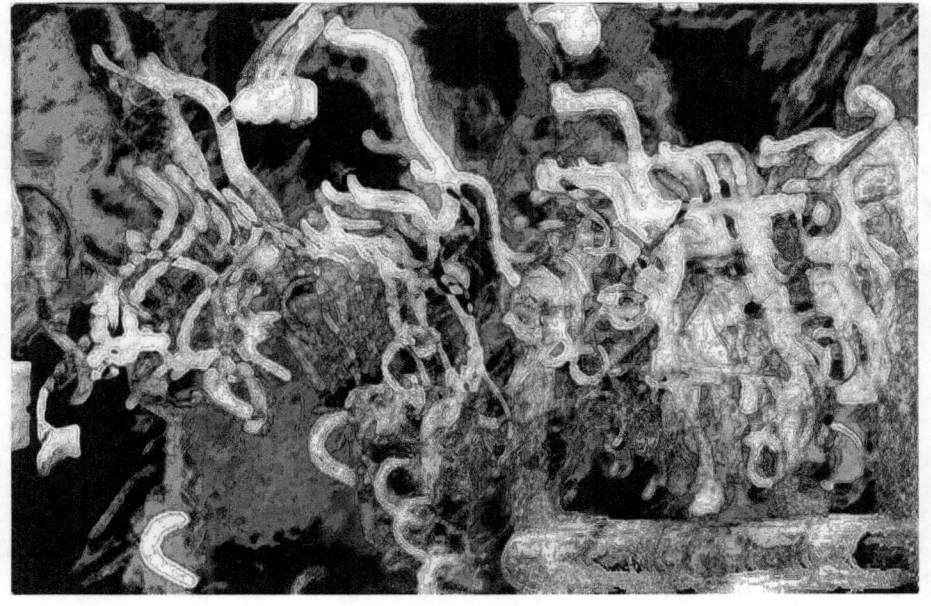

"I managed to get all of my family together at the same time."
"Truly synchronistic, especially since there is only you."

MOTHER AND CHILD

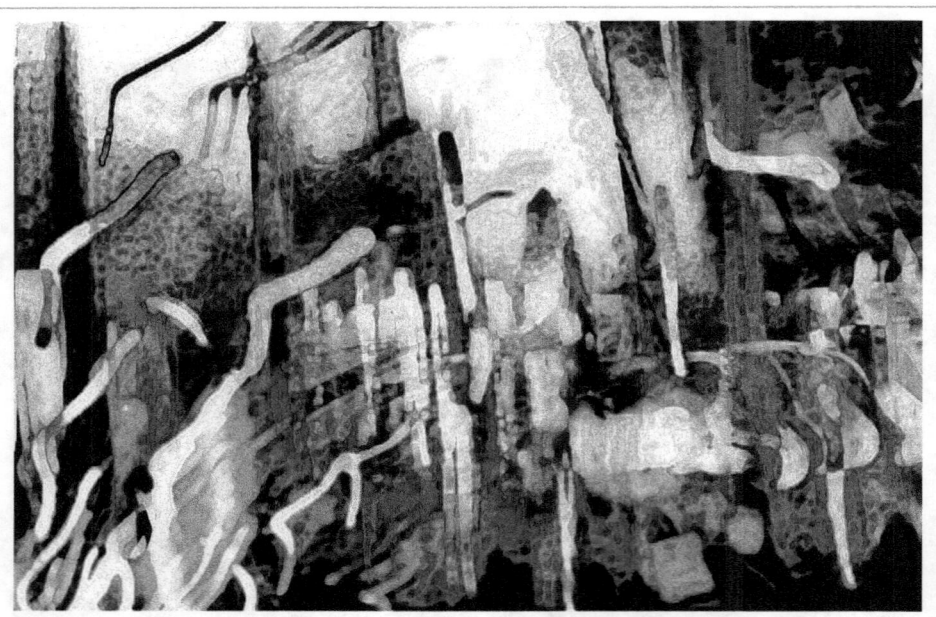

"I am very happy and joyful you are my daughter!"
"And I'm thankful you are my Mom!"

"God Bless."

Index of Print Operas

ADDITIONAL BOOKS BY MISHA HA BAKA

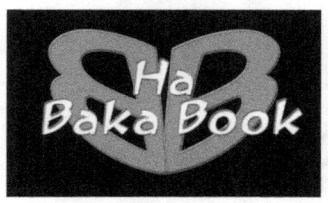

www.habakabook.com

Now that you've enjoyed reading *Two Woman, Three Flamingoes and a Pooch, Two Women Contemplating the Nature of the Universe Print Operas* (in color) and *Two Women Contemplating the Nature of the Universe Print Operas BW* (in black and white) are also available for purchase.

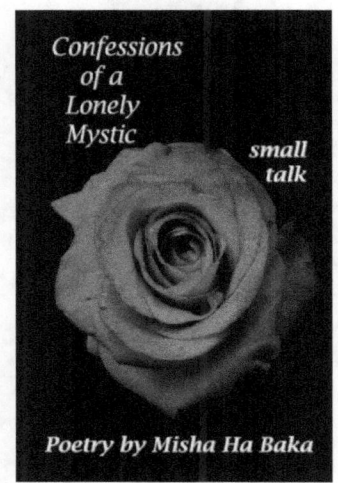

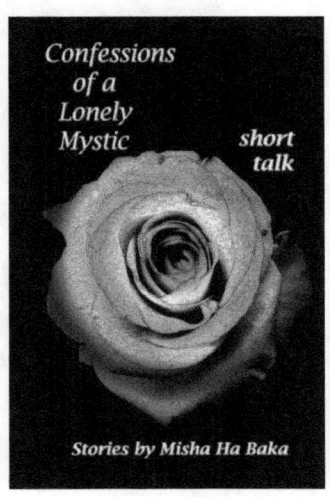

small talk

short talk

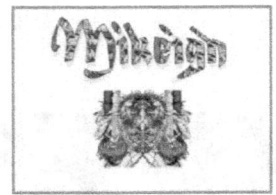

MiKeigh Music

Available for purchase at: www.mikeigh.com.

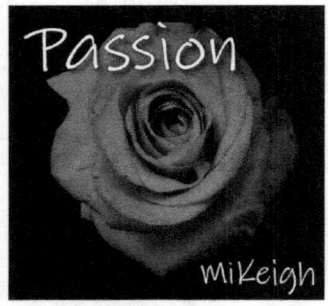

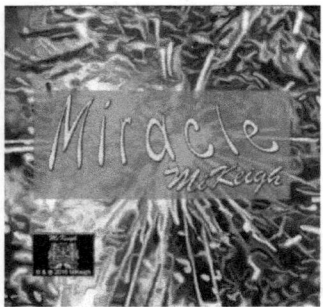

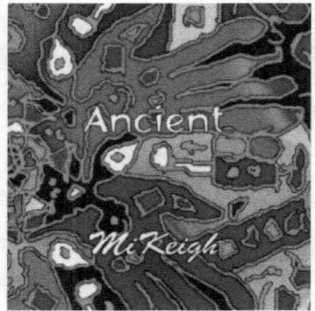

THE LONELY MYSTIC

AS TINY TYKE, THE SAGA BEGINS

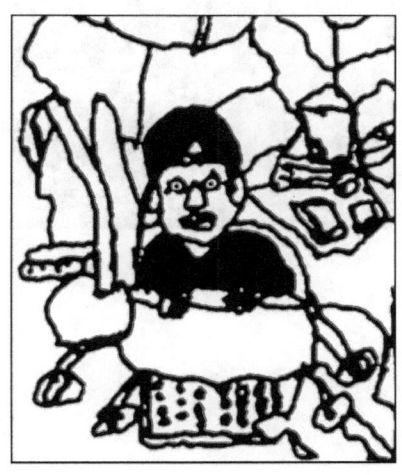

"I'M NOT IN A STROLLER,

THIS IS A HIGH ROLLER!"

EXCERPTED FROM

PORTRAITS OF A LONELY MYSTIC IN 3D

For my beloved wherever she may be…

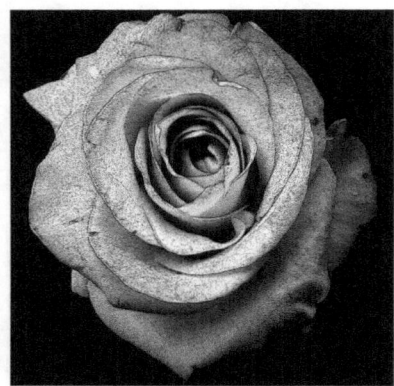

ABOUT THE ARTIST & AUTHOR

Misha Ha Baka has worn many hats during his professional career. He has penned several other works including Confessions of a Lonely Mystic small talk, Confessions of a Lonely Mystic short talk and the illustrated fictional novels series, Portraits of a Lonely Mystic. He holds a BA in English Literature, an MA in Asian Studies and studied healing and mystic thought in Asia, England, Israel, and the United States. He is an ordained spiritual healer and ordained member of the clergy. He is a fine artist, a graphic artist, a photographer, a musician, and a composer with dozens of albums of original music such as *Passion*, *Miracle* and *Ancient*.

Misha Ha Baka books and MiKeigh Music is available for purchase at www.mishahabaka.com, www.mikeigh.com and www.habakabook.com. They are also available for purchase at online retailers and local book sellers.

www.ingramcontent.com/pod-product-compliance
Lightning Source LLC
Chambersburg PA
CBHW072259170526
45158CB00003BA/1115